BUILDING BRIDGES

A POETRY ANTHOLOGY BRIDGING COMMUNITIES

BUILDING BRIDGES

A POETRY ANTHOLOGY BRIDGING COMMUNITIES

RENARD PRESS

RENARD PRESS LTD

124 City Road
London EC1V 2NX
United Kingdom
info@renardpress.com
020 8050 2928

www.renardpress.com

Building Bridges first published in 2024

Cover design by Will Dady

Printed on FSC-accredited papers in the UK by 4edge Limited

ISBN: 978-1-80447-128-9

9 8 7 6 5 4 3 2 1

CONTENTS

ABOUT BUILDING BRIDGES

In February 2021 Renard put out a call for submissions for the New Beginnings poetry project, a competition open to all those who 'felt their voice was silenced in 2020'. We were absolutely overwhelmed by the response to the project, and it became clear how important such open calls are for providing a platform for the voices of those who feel shut out of the mainstream.

In 2022, building on this success, we launched the Spectrum project, followed the next year by Kinship, seeking poems celebrating identity and community respectively. These poetry projects exploring and celebrating diversity and identity have now become a firm fixture in Renard's publishing programme.

This year, against the backdrop of wars raging around the world, and widespread persecution and acts of genocide seeking to eradicate and isolate whole peoples, we chose the title Building Bridges, aiming to celebrate the rich tapestry of humanity and to build bridges across divides with poetry – surely one of the most universal art forms. In your hands you hold the shortlist – an extraordinarily broad, diverse and compelling selection from writers around the world.

As with any project, there were several vital people working away behind the scenes. Miriam Halahmy (who must be credited this year with the great title), Tom Denbigh, Reshma Ruia and Will Dady, the judges, had quite a task whittling down the list to the collection you see here today. Thanks, too, to Hannah Fields, a firm friend of these projects, for her support to date. Thanks must also go to Anna Vaught, who set up the Curae Prize, and Suman Gujral, who spearheaded the Third Space: South Asian Poetry project, with both of whom Renard collaborated to publish anthologies; looking at the contents page of *Building Bridges*, it seems clear that they've been instrumental in helping put some brilliant poets on the map, and our shelves have benefited greatly.

Last but not least, this project was supported by a crowd-funding campaign – thanks in abundance go to all those kind souls who supported the project and, fundamentally, made it possible; their names can be found on p. 137. And finally, our thanks to you, reader, for picking up this book, for supporting this project and, above all, for helping us to celebrate our great networks of community.

THE PUBLISHER

ABOUT THE JUDGES

MIRIAM HALAHMY
Miriam was a teacher for twenty-five years, and, having worked with refugees and asylum seekers in schools, her writing engages with historical and contemporary issues that affect children across time – most notably the plight of refugees. Her young-adult novel, *Hidden*, was a *Sunday Times* Children's Book of the Week, was nominated for the Carnegie Medal and has been adapted for the stage. *A Boy From Baghdad*, Miriam's latest book, is about a boy who is forced into exile to Israel in 1951, with the entire ancient Iraqi Jewish community and the struggle to make a new life in a refugee camp.

TOM DENBIGH
Tom Denbigh is a Bristol-based poet and playwright. Exploring the queer experience alongside tales of friends and strangers, Tom's writing toys with myth, devilish humour and absurdity to portray the bizarre and brilliant in the everyday. He is a producer at Milk Poetry, a BBC1Xtra Words First winner and has facilitated writing workshops for groups of students from the UK and abroad. Outside of poetry Tom has a PhD on plant roots and soil erosion. His first collection *...and then she ate him* is published with Burning Eye Books.

RESHMA RUIA

Reshma Ruia is an award-winning author and poet. She has a PhD and Master's in Creative Writing from Manchester University. She has published two novels (including *Still Lives* with Renard Press), a poetry collection and a short story collection. Her work has appeared in international anthologies and journals, and she has had work commissioned by the BBC. She is the co-founder of The Whole Kahani – a writers' collective of British South Asian writers. Born in India and brought up in Rome, her writing explores the preoccupations of those who possess a multiple sense of belonging.

WILL DADY

Will Dady grew up in the wonderfully named Great Snoring in North Norfolk, and now lives in London. He is the Publisher at Renard Press, which he founded in 2020. A publisher of classic and contemporary fiction, non-fiction, theatre and poetry, part of Renard's raison d'être is to empower and provide a platform to marginalised voices. The New Beginnings project was set up in 2021, followed by Spectrum in 2022 and Kinship in 2023; the huge success in attracting stirring entries has made these projects a firm fixture in Renard's publishing programme.

BUILDING BRIDGES

WINNER

INTERNS AT A FERTILITY CLINIC
Kinshuk Gupta

RUNNER-UP

WHEN YOU GIVE A PLANT TO A TEACHER
Alison Binney

SPECIAL MENTIONS FROM THE JUDGES

MIRIAM HALAHMY

SOURCES FOR THE HISTORY OF BHUTAN
Sekhar Banerjee

TOM DENBIGH

THE SECOND TIME
Max Wallis

RESHMA RUIA

SOURCES FOR THE HISTORY OF BHUTAN
Sekhar Banerjee

WILL DADY

I AM NOT BEAR GRYLLS
Daphne Sampson

KINSHUK GUPTA

Interns at a Fertility Clinic

We have to be quick to dispose of the dead –

hold the pigeon by its oily scarf, mauled
                by the slicked grey blades of an exhaust
fan, its wings spread in a warm welcome.

Clean the pitch-dark carpet of flies whose curled
bodies drift too quickly towards the white light.

Keep our fingers adrift on the trigger of a 0.22
        if we hear a Pomeranian moan,
its white fur dotted with clotted blood.

We paint the walls where anxious women plant their feet
when the doctor shows them swelling and shrinking follicles.

Watch men drop their pants after a quick glance,
        and look suddenly the same – hair and skin
and prune-bellied scrotum.

Our pipettes move like chopsticks as we brush off the cumulus,
make a wreath of sperms around the eggs,

and comment, while peering into the eyepiece,
       on the futility of our race.

Sometimes we think, Why do couples reduce
       their bodies to receptacles, allow pain to hopscotch
through their bodies like a sharp-toothed mouse?

How do they attune their brains to numbers
and percentages, blaming themselves
       for the lives flushed down the drain?

But I remember Roopa aunty, the stretch
of a sarcastic smile on her lips, when she asked chachi
       about kids.

How chachi filled her body to the brim with Pregnyl
and Ovidrel, marking the calendar with red,
waiting for the two red lines to appear on LH strips,
       her hands smelling only of sex for forty-eight hours.

She pressed her sweaty face into the golden-furred dog,
clasped cherry tomatoes like the knobby fingers of a child,
       never allowing them to fall green.

She listened to the sonorous bells of Badrinath for that whole
moonless night,
       prayed for her belly to swell when she saw spotting on the pad.

That night when a limbless child, swathed in blood,
plopped in the green tub, she dreamt of standing on a bridge,
an infant suckling her breasts, not moving

as the bridge burned from both ends.

ALISON BINNEY

When you give a plant to a teacher

We will thank you very much and say
how lovely it will look on our desk.
We will mean it, then pop it on the fridge.
It will be watered once a week, at first,
then maybe once a month, once a term.
It will turn so brown and limp an English teacher
will use it as a prompt. For thirty teenagers,
for an hour, it will become a symbol of hope,
desiccated. Three students will write their
best poem that day. Twenty-seven will
think, It's just a fucking plant, get over it.
Back in the staffroom, it will yield a limb
to soothe a sunburnt PE teacher. An Art trainee
will name it Vera, until a Science technician
will say it should be Alan, actually.
The PE teacher will regret rubbing Alan
on her legs. Alan will outgrow his pot
and be taken home like the class rabbit.
When he returns in a large tub, the head
of Drama will suggest *Little Shop of Horrors*
or the school show. But there will be larvae
in the new compost, and soon break
is bedevilled with flies. Suspicion

must fall upon Alan. He will be banished
to the garden of the pupil referral unit.
No one comes back from there.
He will languish beside beans, gone over,
two gnomes and a plastic hedgehog.
Even then, he will be fine, until the first frost
transfigures his leaves into swords.
He will be borne inside and thawed
with the surplus water from a pot noodle.
The next day, he will resemble a squashed
octopus. There will seem no hope for Alan.
But a teaching assistant will coax a boy
to chop Alan back to his roots with safety
scissors. It's better than Maths anyway,
and as he hacks and swears, he will care
to tip the putrid sap back on the soil,
mumbling about nutrients and shit. And
two months will pass, and no one will think
about Alan, until the teaching assistant spots
lime-green shoots nudging the stump
and sends a photo: 'Is it wrong that it made me
a bit emotional???' When you give a plant
to a teacher, you may think we like to tend,
but we tend haphazardly. What we will do
is notice; what we'll do well is share.

OZ HARDWICK

A Calculated Step

I've left my shoes at the edge of the road,
hung my coat on the horn of a slim moon;
by which I mean it is night and I am lost;
by which I mean that time has slipped away

and I've never strayed so far from home;
by which I mean it's maybe twenty years
since I said home with any real conviction;
by which I mean that, come the morning,

I'll shape myself a nest from spilled words
I find scattered all along the winding way;
by which I mean words shorn of metaphor
and other ambiguities. Take moonlight:

see how it sits like breath on crown glass.
I'll save such signs for tomorrow. By then
my shoes will be nothing but invisible ink
washed from the back of my frozen hand;

by which I mean I'll build a bridge of flowers.

STEVE BAGGS

A man in a bowler hat

This is my face.
A gateway of artistic expression.
I am a brushstroke of life, a whisper growing.
See the distance between us.

I am the unblinking eye.
The spirit speaking in the paint.
I am a hailstorm, a mountain scene,
A grain of frozen graupel.

I am a still life,
The father of a broken silence.
A bather, a cubist, an impression of folding time.
This frame cannot hold me.

I walk snow-blown boulevards at night.
I drink coffee along left-bank cafés.
I swim in the Seine.
I am the bridge between movements.

I am challenging perspectives.
Floating between old and new.
A collection of thoughts.
Connecting the life of art.

I am a mirror inside a mirror,
a reflection of personalities,
a series of portraits of the soul.
A mise en abyme.

Now look again.

CREANA BOSAC

Advice to Interviewers from an
Autistic Candidate

Please switch off any lights
with a high-pitched whine.
This time won't shine for me again.
And please remove the clock
that ticks too loudly
and the crowd –
there's only one of me
so why do you need three?

Ask me any questions
directly and I'll
answer honestly, but please don't
be ambiguous, like
the other times, like
the last time when
I talked about my gran,
which was Wrong (I know now).

I'm not attuned to your
clues of face, pace, tone,
have focus honed sharp on your words.

I can't say where I'll be
in five years' time, no,
no one knows
that, but in scrupulous
preparation I have
many answers
to the questions
you never ask.

HEINRICH BEINDORF

Almost

They worked in rackmaking, speed-weaving
these convoluted heavy-duty
wiring harnesses for a pittance

we called them the Four Graces as
they wafted through the floor aisles
sweet if starkly Oriental in their
Keds & pastel-coloured hijabs

I fancied the middle one, Shabnam
shooting her a look as we sat
sprawled on a stack of pallets by
one of the loading docks

and Matty froze beside me
you bleedin' crazy he hissed
her cousins'll have your neck faster
than you can say Alhamdulillah, mate

then went on to list the demerits and perils
soberly: how you couldn't take a dame like that
to a pub a game a movie an Aerosmith concert
not even camping by the old quarry pond

nor out for a barbecue or a bike cruise
let alone chew politics with her old
man over a pie and a pint

so drop this if you're smart, he said
which I did – I was green then
and the Four Graces stayed inside for their
lunch breaks ever after

though by the chance that rules our lives
I later learnt she married a chef from
the old Osman Bey place who
went on to own two restaurants
and her sons now run a harbour-front
civil-engineering outfit where
I once went to apply for employment

aye, no squabbling over studio time for this girl
no word counts or dodgy narratives
no kidding

so even and especially after all this time
one twigs the issues babe
but still

POET THE JULES

antici-

five minutes before a miracle
happens I sit on the couch
with strapped boots
and my left sock missing
the universe sends me
memos about half-eaten
bowls of oatmeal I'm
kind of tied up right now
about to leave the house
actually but I always have
some room for the
unexpected to sweep
me off my feet especially
on days when my calendar
tries to predict the future
I was told to be ready
yet I don't know what I'm
waiting for all I know is that I
rummaged for bandages
in the bottom drawer
when I found a dinosaur
egg-shaped heart

I let my brain
rest in a fishbowl
sitting on my bedside
table I've been
patiently counting
the hours since we last spoke
festering on your words
so I don't forget what
your voice sounds like
many things are bridges
sometimes the memory of an
embrace can be a boat
carrying me to warmer
days introducing a route
I have not yet discovered
mostly we know what is going
to happen before it does
I find magic in keeping
still listening to the world
spin while clocks start
ticking slower with
every heartbeat until I can
observe my anxiety unfold
in front of me like a jigsaw
puzzle without edges
I shiver with anticipation
for the moments right
before something great
might happen
I hope to meet you

on the other side
but it's
OK if we end up
in different places
I've been
whispering
to the ether
sending this
poem through
space and time
I told you I was
terrified to walk
towards the dreams
I painted in the spaces
between yesterday
and tomorrow
weaving spells in my
bedsheets I drew maps
on the ceiling the nights
I was too tired to sleep
she said not to give
up five minutes before
the miracle happens
since then I've
been calmer not
waiting or expecting
not forceful but trusting
instead of dread I planted
love on my path hope
is my welcome mat

I learned how all
this is a simple
practice you said
you had a lot
of faith
I'm really
glad you let me
borrow some
maybe one
day I get
to return
that favour

KOUSHIK BANERJEA

Art form

In the gloaming, a rat.
Black-tailed divine, living past his dreams
Dumpsters spilling their guts
Lone particle of envy on rodent snout, else invisible the seams
Such abundance, such waste!
Some apron drapes desire
Door cracks open, alley swallows light
Carcinogenic tip scented in the mire

Before the moonlit flit, this Everest of cardboard
He too nursed other ambitions, upright ones in a human form.
Paws sublimely adapted to a phantom world
Stealth shadow the bittersweet of memory
Another life, they numbered three
Before the hole in the ground to match the one in his heart
Love consumed by cruel tongues of flame
Ripped apart

The day it all changed.
Shrapnel wounds empty shell
The past in fragments, mostly living hell
Upright souls hurtling back to earth
Darkness worms coiled string of hate

Coppery red, flesh strewn
Love, heart, remains interred too soon

By night, paws teasing cardboard
Or sliding down the obsidian sheen of bin bags.
Refuse his refuge, nocturnal dare
Burnt, drunk rot twilit call to prayer.
To the true spirits, the ones who sense rat
Flesh of their flesh, public shame laid bare.

Also heard in his plaintive withdrawal
For the stirrings of the heart a lovesick *qawwal*
Ahead of the wound, before the hole
An anytime *raga*. Derided rodent soul

Dark shapes part waste spinning wildly on scrap
Sufi carousel shapeshifting map
Glowing embers waste crackles discarded cigarette
On the ground eye level, the fallen
Bewhiskered dervish, art form in survival
No trash-lit genius, rodent nocturne

Apron departs, darkness regroups, form shudders in the vitals.

THEA SMILEY

As the Last Song Begins to Play

they reach out, their arms spread wide,
curved like wings, to scoop me in.

Dancing alone, coloured lights
spinning around the barn, I back away.

But, after that day – the rising bubbles,
glass flutes clinking in a windy field,

roses tied to the trellis with ribbons,
paper lanterns swinging beneath the trees,

the billowing veil and new blue suits,
warm straw bales and drifting petals,

the clapping flags, rippling bunting,
the flowering flames of fire breathing –

I'm drawn into the circle of dancers
and, with our arms around each other,

we sway in time and sing together:
I don't want to miss a thing

MARK LAVERY

Behind Closed Doors

Remember how they'd gather,
in wooden rooms lit by chandeliers,
Spinning tales of unity, equality and justice for all,
While outside we stood, faces uplifted,
hoping, dreaming, trusting,
Believing their words were more than just pretty shadows
dancing on a hidden cave's wall?

Remember what they told us,
when they sold us visions of a future where we'd soar with untethered wings?
Where our hard work would be fairly rewarded,
and that our children's children's children's children
would, in succession, each live better lives than the generation before?

Remember how they'd step outside when the grain was grown and stored?
Performing plays of patriotism, they spoke of threats beyond our shores.
They saluted flags in uniform, recited oaths from bended knee,
Sent our children off to fight for them, invoking gods none of us could see.

If only then we stopped to ask
Why their hands held all the cards.
Dealing destinies like poker chips,
While we wore all the scars.

Remember how we stood by, witnessing the great divide unfold?
How our voices cried for truth, but deaf ears greeted every plea,
How we sought answers in the depths of their empty, hollow souls,
Only to find echoes of those questions staring back at us and we.

They spoke of bridges, yet burned each plank that reached across the aisle,
Proclaimed unity, but planted seeds of discord deep within our soil,
Fed us slogans instead of substance, watched us fighting for their spoils,
Drawing lines in the sand, carving divisions with calculated toil.

Then, slowly, like waking from a dream woven of moonlit silk,
We realised the charade, the grandest of cons, imposed upon our ilk.
Their promises melting like snowflakes on warm skin, leaving us chilled,
Exposing the naked truth – their throne, perched upon our children's bones.

And so we traded guns for builder's tools,
Broke the chains that bound us tight;
Shattering glass ceilings,
Soon our own bridges took flight.

Spanning aisles, spanning post codes,
Spanning language, colour, creed.
Creating space for all to shine, our creativity freed.

Remember how we toppled giants? How we challenged the sun.
How we carved our names in history, even though we're not yet done.
How we refused to be forgotten, how we sang out our own praise,
For we are the architects of tomorrow, who set the world ablaze.

YUKTI NARANG

Birds and Bones All Live in Houses

A body of performance arts, a tainted mirror, a red lipstick. It takes more than a list to create a persona, and it doesn't die easily. I make friends with a nameless woman, and I see broken bones inside her soft body of honey, and skin, and salt, and veins. She wears casts of white and writes eulogies on them. She sits inside a casket to allow her bones to regrow again. I see that she doesn't look anything like me. Still, I have an undying itch to kiss her, to know her, to name her, even if it is all in my head. When I lean into her, body and mind, I ask why all the cracks in her bones give way so eerily. She haunts me. Birds live inside her fine bones, finding a surreal and warm nest of comfort, an imprint of their lives. One cuckoo bird sits on her tongue, its blue merging with the pink of her mouth. A kind of cotton candy, they dissolve into one another. But soon the birds leave to migrate, flying out through her mouth. Chirping sounds merge into a voice as her bones heal. A house closes up and birds grow up. The woman fixes her mirror and sees smooth red lips gleaming without seeping through shards. I look into that mirror too. And though she speaks to me, my face is a reflection of her. I do not want to name her any more. I want to know her, to kiss her, lean into her. I want her to be real. The looking glass mirrors my shadow, and I wonder if

she was always as important as me. We find each other,
belonging in a big nest. We do not throw another out
when it's weak. We are not songbirds. We are not birds of
prey. We aren't quivering beaks either.

.

REBECCA G. BIBER

Blood and Soil

I come from a family of gardeners, and I the least. No great
carrot swathe, straw-swaddled for the first-frost sweetness. No
tomatoes heavy and hairy with itchy deliciousness, no ripe snap
peas, you get the idea. I grow ground cover that spreads, reliable
orange lilies, shrubs even a crushing snowfall can't kill. The pink
gladiolus volunteered; dusty millers overwintered and I keep them
here.

I refuse to reproduce. The people who made me have accepted this.
My country cannot accept it. Women raised on corn and soybean land
think being female means being them, fecund. Men whose daddies and
granddaddies knew best take up pruners, gloves and fountain pens: first,
pluck decisions from poor women. Cull money already stunted, never
setting foot on parched dirt. Claim to catch accidental infants as they
fall.

But falling fruits have randomness. The breeze. Talk of life ignores
the frail shoot that fails to sprout, to thrive. The blood that rinses
clean. That must be ploughed back in. Not every crop brought forth
next spring will get nourishing rain. Bodies, full or fallow, need more
than law-givers give in their noblesse oblige. Might they look a child
in the eye and say, *Your violation continues now. You will never be
done.*

I come from a fortunate bunch with a little cash. If I needed to rid myself of seed, I would go anywhere. I can. No roots I'd have to saw through, no hothouse beliefs to lose, no squatters' rights on the land, just this little place I call mine alone, within. I will live and die, I will not grow round. I will not insist that others act like me, nor I like them. On my period, I kneel and weed my plot, loath to deracinate anything, unwilling to give up.

DULANI KULASINGHE

Bug at Duckpool

I watch as you wave your legs,
lying on your back, swimming.
No, maybe drowning?

So I break the skin of the rock pool with my finger
but poke you deeper.
Your sudden stillness makes clear

the stakes are higher than I knew.
Scooping you out, I feel
your tiny weight on my palm –

wings half soaked and darkened –
leaving a salt-water trail as you walk
tickling new hairs at finger's base.

You scale my knuckle and – careful climber –
test the slick surface of my fingernail
with your feathery feet.

Somewhere between nail and knuckle, curiosity
slips and love gives you an easy descent, gentles
you back on to barnacled rock.

Dry wings now gold
you make your way
no faster or slower than my hand.

I keep my head low over your progress –
I have a stake in those steps narrowly missed.
I want to see you safe in the world.

SHEENA HUSSAIN

Care Givers on a Break
in a Café

Two are brown, women of faith.
Carla evens them out,
full wet lips, lashes
like bat wings,
silver ear cuff glued
as if gum

The one with the gingham hijab
is on fire –
bitch, she's changed our rota –
as she bites into her omelette wrap
hers is without the Thai green chillies

The pragmatic head amongst them
orders,
Zainab must be washed down
with water,
both after No. 1 and No. 2.
Carla breaks out in fits of giggles –
it's her first time
on the job

Gossip swings like a hanging bar
What did you do?
Tells of a new girl:
new hairstyle, stiff quiff, bling on
all four fingers.
He looked *sick* in her eyes still.
In love

One skipped the morning
prayer.
Tells Carla, *it's not easy being us,*
less than two weeks
we'll be size zeros −
the month of abstinence.
High fives and titters soak the air

Carla is bewitched − vanity a wink
in a compact mirror.
What diet is that then?

IVY RAFF

Collide: Astrophysics in the Time of Genocide by Bombing (and All Other Times)

a found haibun in Neil DeGrasse Tyson

two galaxies collide & leave behind a titanic mess: spiral structures warped beyond recognition, bursts of star-forming regions spawned from violent collisions of clouds. with all this mayhem, how much galactic flotsam permeates space? dark matter doesn't simply consist of matter that happens to be dark. it's something else altogether.

simple algebraic equations
describe attractive force
between any two objects

maybe there's nothing the matter with matter. it's the gravity we don't understand: are we feeling ordinary gravity of ordinary matter crossing membranes of phantom universes adjacent to ours? science measures, preferably with something that's not your own eyes (which inextricably conjoin with the baggage of your brain), a satchel of preconceived ideas, post-conceived notions. dark matter's effects are real. we just don't know what it is.

bright, beautiful, packed
with stars, galaxies decorate dark
voids of space

but just how voidy is the void? without telescopes operating
in multiple bands of light, we might still declare the space
between galaxies to be empty. we probed cosmic countryside,
revealed all manner of hard-to-detect things: runaway stars,
runaway stars that explode, dark matter, faint blue galaxies,
super-duper high energy charged particles, mysterious
quantum vacuum energy. one could argue all the fun in the
universe happens between galaxies rather than within them.

matter we have come to love – stuff
of stars, planets, life – only light
frosting on the cosmic cake

modest buoys float in vast cosmic oceans of something that
looks like nothing. the very word galaxy derives from milky
– cloudlike splotches on the sky. galaxies that no longer
manufacture stars? tiny, boring smudges. but since they
outnumber normal galaxies, our definition of normal needs
revision. dark matter neither absorbs nor emits nor reflects
nor scatters light. it exerts gravity according to the same
rules ordinary matter follows, but does little else to allow us
to detect it.

we remain content to carry dark
matter along – invoking it
when the universe requires

DAVE WYNNE-JONES

Dragon Lines

I imagine the shades of Du Fu and Wordsworth,
in whatever afterworld they might inhabit,
comparing cottages once shared with friends
and family, the curious birds that peeped
through window frames by hills or rivers,
monasteries or abbeys, ruined or not,
the damp, overgrown hedges, wicket gates
in need of maintenance to keep out livestock,
nights spent calling to owls across a lake
or filled with gibbon shrieks from steep gorge walls.

They'd gossip about neighbours, characters,
local peasants or gentry, whose burdens
of poverty or disastrous war, foreseen
or unforeseen, endorsed integrity
or led to betrayal; tales in common
speech energised by shaping powers
in rocks and stones and trees, speaking
as peasant-poets, ballad-makers
sharing the experience of suffering
in poverty or tidal swells of war,
lives rooted deeply in the land they lived on.

Inevitably they'd compare effects
of opium or alcohol that helped
or hindered Coleridge or Li Po
to be friends, philosophers and poets,
distracted from Xanadu or dunked in rivers,
the painful partings and reunions;
debating then the dignity of exile,
the merits of travel, eddying on
down rivers, inconclusively passing
a ship that sank like lead although without
drowning the memories of lost children.

Turning to their time in public service,
reserving for themselves a little
self-consciousness, perhaps self-mockery,
aware of the personal cost of sinecures,
disengaged by then from politics' intrigues
that offer or threaten some security,
which only Wordsworth found, although Du Fu
sang and danced in his decrepitude.

Two minds, a thousand years apart, converge,
confide in poems those revelations
perched high on outcrops in evening light,
above currents of wind and rippling water,
or undulating gorges, mountain ridges,
where Dragon lines wreathe still or wave-chopped lakes
in sun or storm with power, finding a Way
to lay up store, amongst dull pavements grey,
of visions so much more than memory –
sharing the burden of the mystery.

Early Risers Constellation

This poem is for you, Eileen, who gathers up last night's broken glass
outside the pub, fearless, a dancer once, in your eighties now;
for Dot, tidying weeds in the churchyard, restless,
seeking respite from a sick man and too-small rooms;
for Jack, whose dogs are family, parka hood always up,
old sailor of merchant ships, wild, womanless;
for Sarah, lover of political conversation, who spoils
her grumpy wire-haired terrier with Sunday dinners every day:
after my husband died I couldn't sleep,
found a rescue dog for company who was an early riser too
and every morning since, summer, winter,
we've found you, circling the still village,
companion stars on our set course, my secret family.

LJ IRETON

Feet under the Brontë Falls

There is a waterfall in Yorkshire,
in-between moors strewn with thorns –
that pours champagne for the soul,
the pilgrim walker.
Before it was named after her,
Charlotte called it *perfect*,
beautiful and white –
to my eyes, the moss and rush and root
were the grey-green dawn of time,
a D.H. Lawrence poem.

From the veil, the exhale,
the water flows into a ravine,
winding around hardy wildflowers
sprung up through tumbled-down rocks.
It hums slower here –
where each traveller has gathered for miles and centuries,
discarding shoes, socks and cities –
to sit, as we do, like dust-stained dinner guests
around a sacred table;
with soil in our fingernails from climbing
and bramble-scratched skin.
But the invite is instinctual;

our fingers and legs dip in
to the ethereal-turned-tame thing –
joining pebble and ritual, poetry roaming copper
whetting our minds, the dry horizon.

I thought of the sisters once stepping genius
where I swirled my toes – many of us come to see the ghosts
of gothic anti-heroes and their writers.
But the ancient brook, the bush, the oak is older than them –
the beginning heart of always-water
giving a vision of old earth.
We all get to touch it – however we were called here –
our feet are cleaned in the same stream
under the same story-making sun.

ANSUYA

God Talks

They say God talks to us
through people. Notting Hill is full
of God. On Sundays, every step

I'm offered flyers with smiles.
Jesus loves you.
He loves you too, I reply.

In Pret two skinny boys sniff around
ham and cheese toasties, slip them up
their tops and grab Cokes

on their way out. A lady in pearls
and pink lips enters like a Botticelli
painting for a full-fat Danish.

Lucky me, she says. She eats it like
manna from heaven.
The-seven-days-a-week guy tips his hat

at every face he knows, sips and slurps
coffee from a beaker, taps away on his
keyboard, *shot a darling*, he yells.

Opposite me is a live sermon being recited.
Jesus loves you, he wants to know you.
A face turns to me.

Sure I'd like a one-to-one, if he's free now.
I'll save a fortune on therapy.
We can pray together some time, he says.

God has a funny way of reaching me.
Two girls share my table, offer me ginger
cake. I follow them into their evening

of live music and dance welcomed by
a world of faces under the roof of heaven.
I leave smiling into Monday.

EMILY REYNOLDS

Holding on

You are pressing
the tips of my fingers
into the hammock
of your hands
We lie separate
connected
by this delicate bridge
arms outstretched
thumb and finger
a pocket into which
I'm tucked
You think I'm asleep
on the grass
from the pressure
of your grasp
I know you're not
but I don't speak

Before I knew
who you were
it was easier to kiss
than to talk
words, uncomfortable

stepping stones
to fall from
an embarrassing slip
but eyes closed
lips together
not together
a safer way
to know you

DAPHNE SAMPSON

I Am Not Bear Grylls

I am not Bear Grylls

but believe you can make
strong connections
from lianas or other fibres;
perhaps even strips of fabric
can be knotted to make ropes.

Wheelchair immobility
less irksome
when spiced with memories
of youthful travels –
made vivid by boxes of dog-eared photos
and a wardrobe shelf
piled with fabric lengths,
tactile mementos.

Facing a week's respite stay
in a care home,
new to me,
some trepidation –
not real fear,
far from the gut-wrenching

of looking down from a height
past your feet
to a torrent below –
just dull anxiety.

So much that is so intimate
with this new cast –
will we manage the complex choreography,
the transfers from bed to chair
to toilet and back?
Will simply being there
depress me,
the sad calls of other residents
puncture the flimsy balloon of my spirits?
Not being able to reach out
across the chasm of dementia distress?

Now I'm here, long nights with slow dawn hours
lit with sweet daydreams of travelling
unravelling with darker dreams of myself coming apart.

A bright morning knock at my bedroom door;
carers' hands holding me gently but tight,
the knots in a rope bridge.

Amidst election soundbites,
it's the geographical scatter
of the carers' origins
that raises me –
a scatter of bright flowers
in this dull meadow.

Ma from Thailand,
tiny and tough,
as slight as a single
Bangkok silkworm thread.
Strong and stalwart,
but cheering too,
as the long scarlet and gold scarves
in a noisy market.

Elegant Amina from Nigeria –
her laughter and delight
in my memories
of Kano and Lagos
fifty-one years ago,
spanning not just miles
but time.
I see long strips of blue indigo
Kano tie-dyed cloth
still with the raw whiff of the dye-vat.
The blue rubs off on my hands,
grasping these ropes gratefully.

Finally, a special joy,
Natalie from Kenya,
working to fund a degree course
back home in Nairobi.
Indulging my bravest efforts
to recall Kiswahili.
More laughter
lifting my spirits.

She would, of course,
bring me the brightest kanga cloths
from her Kenyan coast,
complete with Swahili proverbs,
Daraja ukilibomoa ujue kuogelea
(If you destroy a bridge, be sure you can swim),
passed from person to person
now often worn soft and thin, translucent
as early morning cloud burning away in hot sun.

I step off the end of the week,
legs shaky but heart high.
No jute here – but against the odds,
those fine fibres of silk and cotton
held me safe,
a hint of more magic to come –
dreams of mothballing my wheelchair.

TIM KIELY

I have heard
that in some languages

what we call a 'poem'
is a collection of cut flowers
                              when I heard
that the tree at the end of my street had revealed
its wax-white leaves I needed to see it
for myself I left my apartment

when it was still dark walked past the tumbled
front gardens of my neighbours
                              a 'poem'
is a well-arranged heap of stones I approached
with the sun ahead of me under dark clouds
looking exactly like a thought

still crouching somewhere in the brain to discover
that I was not alone
                              a 'poem'
is a litany of significant lives there were people
already in the streets sweeping up
to the steps of the town hall like a forest

their anger went before them like
a pillar of fire in the night
                    a 'poem'
is coals placed into the mouth they shouted
and around them the whole town resounded
I almost believed that the crowded living

and the dead were together
demanding what was theirs
                    a 'poem'
is an explosion in a crowd the howls
of the dispersal sirens the hammer
of all the water cannons did

eventually clear the streets
that continued to ring for hours
                        a 'poem'
is a silencing cover of snow I walked
the echoing streets until the sun hung
straight over my head like a sword the air

still carried their cries nothing could claw back
what they in their ghosthood claimed
                        a 'poem'
is a crudely constructed shelter I stopped
at the top of the shopping parade and my ribs
were full of wax-white leaves

                    a 'poem'
is a scarecrow facing the sky
                    a 'poem'

is a mushroom erupting from rot

                              a 'poem'
is an agonised escape

the next day over coffee and cake
my sister asked me what it would take
for me to write poetry again I laid
my coffee cup aside leaned back
as if I might get up and leave I crossed
my arms before the crumbs and newspapers

as if any of this added up to a poem

GERALD EWA

In the kitchen of the world

we gather around a huge mahogany table. we clench our tools: a spoon, knife, plate, grater. our eyes shimmer with expectations as we dissect dead dreams as though to wake them up. we empty our dreams in a large pot simmering on a stove. the powdery blue sky beside the window winks at us. we cringe as the oil hisses and a thin smoke curls into the air. we arch our backs. we welcome the ghost of the past. we cry at the thought of every failed relationship. we number the betrayals and tend the wounds. we count the stars in our eyes and remember how to smile. we forget what it's like to carry many nights in watery eyes. we laugh until we feel the sun in our bellies dappling through the gardens. we are fearless, reckless. we raze down walls impeding our steps. we set new terrains. we sow seeds; we sigh at those plans that may never sprout from the earth. we toast to an unbound life. we eat. we belch. we dance. we grease our weathered palms with oil and watch them bloom again. we glow. we want to carry tomorrow without its many demands. we try to sing the scars away. we fail. but we don't cry. we wait for the night to greet.

HANA ORMARA

Legends of the Sun:
A Hybrid Ghazal of Migration

written to honour the bravery
of all migrants

Drought

Born to love and desire, born to a blazing sun. Where thirst and hunger burned entire generations. A land on fire with starvation is a lethal gun.

On a different horizon – a different sun.

War Shadows

Unseen daggers, bombs and rifles bare their teeth for fun, to delight in pebbles thrown from just a younger one. Skimming shadows, are legends with all their sons.

A globe fleeing the darkness cries out for the sun!

Brothers

Brothers stretched their sights to shores and both in hope they swam. Loss made dusk of every dream and drowned a dawn at once.

Please hold dear in every breath the heartbeat of the sun.

Noor

I am not from outer space, I'm not an alien. I'm not the animal of a French jungle, I am a migrant. I am Noor, the light, I'm striving for my Zion;

and I'm a human standing here, to reach out for the sun!

A Carpenter Prays

Crossings crossed in journey's made, let's honour all and one. In our vessels must be love beyond material sum. For legends lost and for survivors, Omid[1] has won.

In this act of pure belief – don't we become the sun?

The Earth

I am Dounia, the world, daughter to all and one. Made of earth and of water in communion, but my senses were bound by reigns of destruction;

so I broke free – to soar and orbit, right around the sun!

A Poet's Legacy

Here are people, moving, to turn the earth and to live in the abundance of their right of birth. I heard from a great poet this is freedom's song; he said:

'No one – no one – can stop the sun.'

1 Omid means 'Hope' in Persian.

DELILAH DENNETT

Memoria

Pappy bundles me into
Coat scarf hat gloves winter boots
Mummy doesn't like me wearing those
Pappy's good lady friend got me them
All white and brown I'm a plump Christmas pudding
Ready for eating
A steaming dumpling
An egg on legs!
Come on come on Pappy says
Waddling my way to the car
We're going to see Nanny Cole
My pappy's mum's mother
She's ancient
She's a million years old
She's a mummy without the wrapped around loo roll
And when she kisses you it stains your cheek
Zombie spit
Poison

We're rolling along
A red wheewhaw whirring past
Pappy puts a middle finger up to another man driving his car
He shouts at me when I copy him

We arrive and Nanny Cole comes out
She's alive she's alive!
They both tell me to shush
I'm on the wooden chair
My bum is aaaaaaaching oweee
I'm kicking my heels against the legs
Spiders are crawling up!
Pappy garumphs and guffaws
Telling me to be quiet
And I am
Quiet as a mouse
Nibble nibble nibble
Nanny Cole doesn't like mice
She's got traps everywhere
She doesn't want them in the house
All because she doesn't want to feed them

Nanny Jackie said that we are Jewish
I don't really know what that means
Funny hats big hats
Singing a lot in strange voices
Are we Jewish Nanny Cole? Are we?

And she says
What did she say what did that girl say I'm not Jewish
I'm not
I'm not

Pappy coos at her
She's just a kid she doesn't know what she's talking about
He flaps at me with his other hand

Shoo shoo at me a pigeon
Off I dawdle
Into the garden
Everything's dead now in winter.

GEETHA NAIR G.

Memories of Matriarchal Days

I remember the old homestead so well!
The mossed tiles broken in parts,
The dark dank rooms echoing to our tread,
The big swing in the boudoir where Great Aunt sat topless,
Pendulous breasts flung backwards over shoulders to ease the May heat…

She would tell of times when HER mother reigned,
Lovely as a white water lily;
The three men, her transient sleeping partners
Who gave her the schoolmaster, the soldier,
And herself, the girl who didn't take a man.

'Life has been good,' she would say, folding a betel leaf into a cone.
'No one berated my unwed state,
No one hurt me the way Neeli's drunken husband beats her…
There is always enough rice in the barn
And coconuts in the lean-to,
Milk and buttermilk to drown in – see how many cows
Crop grass in our meadows!
And the southern corner of the grounds awaits me,
With three solid nephews to carry me there
And perform my last rites aright.

And there's Ammini, my dear maid,
To light the lamp at dusk before my select bones…'

Great Aunt, what would you make
Of your brothers' granddaughters,
Grown old now,
Each in her cell,
Widowed, separated or divorced,
Neatly snipping Milma packets each morning
Hoping for a neat electric cremation?

Mumbai's new
bridge

Afterwards, we drive over the length
of the new bridge, its curve like
an armful of flowers, and gaze
at the diamonds in the Arabian sea.
Ahead, the hologram of urbanity expands
like a promise, linking dreams
to the soul. One can only marvel
at the speed of progress in the
evening light, in which even the blue
tarp of need is made picturesque by the
sun's wet kiss. As we cruise on to another
limb, metal and cement grow familiar
under the fuchsia sky. My father begins
to ruminate on a vow fulfilled
in his lifetime, and the
imbalance from which came this
moment of awe. To one end
are our lives: a melding of
gold and survival, while the other
holds hope. Between them lies this
wish over which aspirations

now soar like comets. Sitting beside
my father, listening to him accept
his mortality, I hold on to our
proximity, and focus, like him,
on the direction of love.

MWENDIA MURIITHI

My Boy's Blood

He was stood
waiting patiently for the bus
and I was waiting for him at home
preparing his tea
but he never came home that night
because my boy's blood
instead stained the street.

He was only walking back from the library
the CCTV cameras show his face was
filled with innocence and glee
but his body grew cold in a dirty
derelict staircase
because my boy's blood
instead stained the street.

He was only coming back
from a night at the pub
didn't have that many
drinks maybe two or three
but a blow to the head
meant he never smiled at me again
because my boy's blood
instead stained the street.

He told me just yesterday what his
favourite show was and all he wanted
to one day achieve
but I'll never get to say I love you again
nor tuck him in to sleep
because my boy's blood
instead stained the street.

VICTORIA D'CRUZ

My Mother's Tongue

Sometimes, now only very rarely, will I dream in my mother's language. Only here I understand it all and talk confidently in my everyday personality, making jokes and people laugh.

Sometimes, now only very rarely, will I think to myself in my mother's tongue, remembering something from before the last generation who didn't any speak English were around.

Sometimes, now only very rarely, will I remember the me who speaks in my mother's words, shyly and quietly in case I wake the Viking who still lives inside of me.

Sleeping.

MARÍA CASTRO DOMÍNGUEZ

My uncle said we all
needed someone to remember
that we lived

J repeats his parent's stories
over and over; I press my ear to them
keeping them close
his half-fiction recruiting me.

The ghost of his mother lingers for days
a yellow hairband tangled with her grey hairs.
She had locked him up for life
twisted in the vice of familiar touch.

J's father also finds his way back
to the moon of his stories.
He carried J on his shoulders, taught him
to swim wild against the tide.

With J's periscope I can see above
a mother's silence. Her purple lips thinning
after J moved out with yet another friend
yet she'd bake his favourite cake when he returned.

I can see Father's humour illuminated.
His green tweed cap reeking of tobacco.
He'd go to church every Sunday
then shoplift for the poor *like himself*.

I don't want J to end his stories
it's like a new grief all over again.
I want his mother and father wrapped
around us like a rich blue blanket.

RACHEL BURNS

No Apologies

I apologise to the GP for my body.
Yes, he says, your body is a lot.
And I laugh all the way to work,
driving my beat-up car,
singing along to Chaka Khan,
lanyard swinging from my neck.

I sit my body down in the surplus food café.
Susan makes her way through the throng,
carrying her chronic pain body
in a string bag.

Everybody squeezes together like family.
On a trestle table, loaves of white bread
and bunches of blackened bananas.
Help Yourself scrawled on the sign.

A marmalade of young women,
hair blazing vibrant pinks, blues and reds,
lay down their crutches
like a protest across a table.

In the corner sits Mick, sad in his body.
Stares at an empty banana skin,
places it on top of a wooden spoon
table number to make a golden-haired puppet.

Susan says she can't even walk her body
across a room, never mind leave the house.
Alan says to her, gently, I'm the same.
Then everyone chips in like kind aunties.

And Carol, new to the group,
says she wakes up in pain
and she can't get up for work.
I mean, I can't actually move! she laughs,
and we all laugh and nod in agreement,
as if to say, Welcome B-o-d-y.

ALYSON SMITH

Others Meanwhile Are
Neurodivergent

I began to emerge[1]
Straight into diversity[2]
And safe validity[3]

---

1 Aided by the internet
   autistic people
   were able to connect
   and began sharing
   their experiences.

2 Others meanwhile
   are neurodivergent
   with brains that are built
   and work
   somewhat differently.

3 In the UK
   at least one per cent
   of people
   are said
   to be neurodivergent.

ALICE EAVES

Our Lady Star of the Sea

In her silence you tear up the riverbed
snake a path from the water's mouth
deep into the veins of the city
a grey-scape of factory floors
where children's lost fingertips stoke the fires

In her silence you reclaim the swamp land
and announce it our home
stomping over chicks' nests to erect
a brick house on shifting sands
wondering why it slips in the night

In her silence you take your boats
out into the riptides wielding a
titanium rod the length of a town
and plunge it into the seabed
licking black gold from your lips

In her silence you bulldoze caramel dunes
to plant technicolour parasols like toothpicks
plucking the remainder of pampas grass,
bug skins and bird feet
from your waning enamel

In her silence you dig into the soil with hammers
force cracks in the tarmac
drill the meadows until they shriek
so normalised we struggle to sleep
without the white noise of rocking floorboards

In her silence you drip-feed plutonium
into our breakfast cereal, corral us into a pen
of nuclear fission, put us down like ponies
when tumours pulse in our flesh
rather than turning off the television

In her silence you build jets that fly
lower, shout louder over the bay
offering big money to human bots
happy to sell their souls to the manufacture
of civilian-killing war machines

In her silence you ignore the screams of the sea
the skeletons of her children
washed up on driveways
continue to swing incense at her porcelain feet

Our lady has seen you rip apart islands
burn whole nations to the ground
and you dare to ask her for protection
by slipping a wafer under your tongue

LINNEA

Queer Skin

I remember being six
Playing on a beach
Strange adult men joking
About how much they would pay for me

I was ten at the corner store just up the road
When the clerk stroked my face with the back of his hand
And no matter how much we needed toilet paper or tea
I never wanted to go back

I remember being twelve
All lined up for class, still early in the day
When the tall boy went down the line
Asking me if I liked girls that way

I remember when we were fourteen
Shy behind our desks
The small lady came in and talked to us about what it means to say yes
I remember how we laughed, I couldn't stop myself
And then the boy I liked said it depends on how we're dressed

I remember being a little older
And still feeling young

And how my sister's friend pulled me on to his lap for a photograph
And it wasn't a big thing
It was just me being young
Still feeling strange about unwanted touch

But when someone touches me now
And I feel hollow
When I start to feel good
And then fall in
And can't stop the circles of dark in the heavy eyes that do the seeing
When I can't make sense of it
And it slips past me
It's because I know I am lucky
That I've had it this easy.

I saw the tall boy a week ago
He's much taller now and wore a suit and shiny leather shoes
I told him about the person I love most

I'll call them Lola

Because I think maybe the thing about the darkness
Is the same as the boys and their tallness
Is the same as Lola
And the things Mum told me
And whether or not I am angry

And even though it feels strange to journey through sleepless
dreams for the sake of things that are only me
I am me when I am touched, when I am loved, when it is dark, and
night and morning

I am me when I watch my phone, hear the radio, the TV
I am me when I protest, and listen and learn,
When I am given another chance to say no
When I can stand for all that falls in my name because of the
things I did not know to care for a few weeks ago

Because in knowing Lola
I know love in a way I didn't before
I know the way they know me
And the way I know them
I think I understand better why we are so scared
And because of it, I know hope now
Hope that isn't pretending
Hope that laughs and dances and cries a lot
Hope that cries so much it shakes and gets a runny nose, and
says too much on long calls on the phone
I know what it's like to believe it when someone says they love me
I know what it's like to not want to stay here
I know I am so grateful that I can be

SUJATHA MENON

Riptide

In the seventeenth century, birthmarks were sometimes called 'longing
marks', supposedly demonstrating the pregnant mother's longing for
something before her baby was born.

Amma was looking for nits in the baby's blessing of hair
that would one day flap like the flag of England.

She had not stepped off a plane for some years now or
recently recoiled from other children

so what she was really searching for was inspiration to crawl
through the darkness, back home to the breast of the motherland.

The baby's skin skimmed its soft bones so perfectly but gave no story
in the shape of a palm or a bird or dark island off the coast

of a continent shrinking. Instead Amma sang songs through the blanket
of night, tracing long ships with her voice

and her baby's head with an anchored finger:

Savitri, Savitri, Savitri, Sarvatra, Sarvatra, Sarvatra
Savitri, Savitri, Savitri, Sarvatra, Sarvatra, Sarvatra

JASPREET MANDER

Sara

As I walk the long drive
to the portico and
semi-circular reception
of the academy
there she is
Sara – the tuck-shop girl
in a corner to the left
standing on her high chair
behind the counter
she beams and waves
as she sees me
warmth rippling through her frame
from the top of the plaits to
the buckles of her shoes

mornings afford no more
than a brisk hello
dash to teachers' vestibule
my locker and lessons for the day
translation extracts
précis, paragraph writing
synonyms, collocations
loads of grammar

subject–object complement
Blake's 'The Clod and the Pebble'
Byron's 'The Prisoner of Chillon'
Kamala Markandaya's *A Handful of Rice*
David Copperfield abridged
year after year
some of the above leave
new ones come in
and so it goes on

year after year
Sara, with her sister Ruby,
stocks up the tuck shop
sheds a few things that stay unsold
brings in those in demand
chocolate bars, éclairs, ice lollies
smarties, choco-chip biscuits, carrot cakes
jim-jams, pipped dates
ribbed crisps, super-spicy crisps
loads of fizzes
diaries, lined notebooks, notepads
ballpoint pens, gold gel pens,
markers, glitter pencils
scratch cards for raffles and lottery

Friday afternoons
our chat times, Sara and mine
little to big things under the sun
Sara talks of difficulties with jargon
in her electives – sociology and history
so much that teachers assume

their pupils know and understand
while they remain clueless
the slow pace of her writing
when everything boils down
to the three-hour written exam
the low chairs she needs
not available nearly always
the near-stampede on staircases and corridors
she has to avoid
Ruby's delayed diagnosis – scoliosis –
getting worse by the day
the scandalised grimaces
she encounters every single day
hordes of ugly looks – sine qua non of her life
life at home after Mum and Dad
had passed away intestate
property matters and aliens
of older brothers
patriarchy and misogyny
as ever, the familiar twin swords

I speak of pressures at home
the slogan repeats ad infinitum
every single day
settle down and do
as the wont of the world
the eligible men I'm made to meet
the botanist, the PE teacher
betel-chewing judge – worst of the lot
my words subdued in disbelief
as the question hour shoots up

I in the dock
man-surveyor in judge's chair
the most recent specimen
wants to know how I do
dishes and laundry
refusing to budge when asked to leave
and I wonder if I'll have to
push him down the garden, out the gate

Five years after I left the academy
Sara's words and warmth
continue to assuage the hurts and harm
that hurtle
my way and hers
inevitable, they say, for women
of all girths and lengths

Two of Sara's conversations
etched on my heart
to my dying day
my talisman

A ringing voice arrives from nowhere
can't see anyone
I look around more searchingly
the pitch-pipe tone says hello again
this time I look to my left
right, front, back
but also further back
and there she is

Her warm voice chortles, 'Hello'
'Hello,' I say, in a fluster and out of depth
I try and bend
realise soon I'll have to bend fairly low
to be level with the supple tones
she smiles, 'Please don't bend double
to take my hand
you might get a backache
you don't have to but you can
kneel safely and take my hand
without a stiff back in the making'
'Ohh ohh, I... I get it,' I stammer
I kneel awkwardly
extending my hand limply
she puts her pudgy little hand in mine
'I am Sara
all of nineteen'
'I'm Mehreen
just joined the academy
will be teaching English literature
and language'
'Lovely to meet you
my sister, Ruby, and I
run the tuck shop here
everyday eats and other things
for pupils
our father set up this shop
now it's us
by the way, I am all of
two feet and eight inches
but Sara every inch'

And later, one day

'I don't mind dwarfism, Mehreen
they can call me
a dwarf, a midget
I am one'
'Why should you not mind?'
'What's there to mind?
it's a fact
though they can make do with
short stature or
persons of restricted growth
I think many are not aware
of what they say
and the rest don't bother
to evolve their vocabulary'
'Why don't you tell them off?'
'No point
most can outshout me'
'And so?'
'Well, it's just physical dwarfism
for me
it could have been
emotional, mental or social dwarfism
would have been worse
much, much worse
and so, I'm happy the way I am'

KAY SAUNDERS

Settle over Satiate

Eden grew like love on the horizon as the city shrank in my
rear view; ten and two,
sweaty hair and a sound like a loose marble in the bonnet,
asphalt to sand, swollen eyes, aching chest –
my phone with zero missed calls.

Eden beckoned me with maple and oak and wisteria
on white brick, tall grass, dust in the
grooves of my shoes, ice cubes, cigarette butts,
strawberry tunnels, green bar stools,
a girl with red-wine hair and a camper van.

Eden told me, 'Let go or be dragged back to
where you came from', so I held tightly to the
strap of my backpack, leather reins, beer bottles,
door handles; anything to keep my searching
hands busy, distracted, away from skin and skirts and
the scab I can't stop scratching.

Eden was an island with no shore and no ending;
a feeling, a lighthouse with two porches and a patio,
ten chairs and another three
stacked in the corner, a six-string guitar – a mother

so unlike my own with mirth and mud on her
nose and a father that treated me like a daughter.

Eden handed me a shotgun with a shining barrel and a pair
of brown boots, an oversized
flannel, a pair of kitchen scissors to keep my hair
short at the back; a bed with gingham sheets, a chair by an
open window where the draping swelled with a merciful breeze
and a clean toothbrush.

Eden pulled me underwater by my ankle;
the lakebed, a patchwork of pebbles and a forgotten bracelet,
can tabs, copper coins, led me to the bank and an open palm,
that girl with the red hair and the van −
she stripped me bare and I helped her with the buttons.

Eden did not ask where I had been when I came in and
kicked off my shoes, and my coat;
a stranger, city-boned, queer and resistant and bitter and a liar;
Eden only said, 'You are here now, so why should it matter?'

SEKHAR BANERJEE

Sources for the History of Bhutan

Let's say Phuentsholing is a tired filament
of an old bulb. But you know every town
is a worn-out filament of delight
late into the night, yellowed.
Though Buddha never told us to differentiate
too much between a butter lamp
and a Thomas Edison bulb, or a day and a millennium
or a storksbill and a blue geranium,
our incandescence is a yellow filament shrouded
in a day's emptiness. Count zillions into that
province. A person, a day's yellow summery.
A day is an ambered millennium.

A bulb or a geranium, whoever you are, you are always
prone to have a Friday evening on your face,
the weekend, and make earnest rounds and rounds
like a highland yak around merriment
and the cottage cheese smell – the scent of the mountain
Buddha, in the small hour between night and the morning
in a small town,
praising everything that turns us salubrious –
the beverage, the climate,
the groggy town, the hum of Bhutanese songs on the radio,

the sources of adequate mirth, or the young bartender
because Saint Aquinas foretold beforehand that men
want happiness, women too.

Though we have seen fish swallowing
inundation, like us,
and releasing buoyancy, and birds inhaling the troposphere
and exhaling flights.
We are no exception to that. We need to stuff
the entire history of gladness inside some fluffy evenings
like field notes in June
in Phuentsholing or any other small town, in any other
country, inside a sultry dusk inside
an early summer and fall fast asleep before our next birth.
But you cannot fall asleep because it is not easy
to fall asleep in the middle
of a confusing tiger-donkey year
everywhere on earth, and the last bus to Chapcha
or, for that matter, to every place that has left before the evening –
another millennium –
and a husky rain starts falling on the fallacies
of history
in a mountain town at the ankle of the Himalayas.

CARL GRIFFIN

The Allotment Pharmacy

The veg lady –
        white hair and sulphurous
                        garden clothes
            turning her into an overboiled
                        cauliflower –
marshals us on a tour around patches
blighted with ground frost.

        Folk say
the allotments are designed like a hospital
                        dispensary,
that medicine lies in the steaming heaps –
it's the organic matter of the soil.

She bends with oiled joints
                        alongside allotmenteers
and tugs at frozen red peppers.
I call these horizons, she smiles.
They do wonders for the blood vessels
                        in plodding eyes.

Almonds grow here, and walnuts. I call them hurdles,
she says, when we point to the trees.
The fatty acids mend a broken back.

My twenties something wanders off.
    I confess to our guide
    my arthritic hands,
        how they stiffen,
            impersonalise
            our sexual gymnastics
    or make washing dishes
    an impossible task.
And when the lad hobbles back
    he exaggerates
    his blistered feet,
        fusses over his strained thighs
        and sore ankles.

But the ice! Now everything looks like cauliflower!

I lower my voice to my midlife crisis,
    Did we tithe enough, do you think?
And while he grimaces at the possibility
the lady laughs off our superstition.
    She ferrets out various whitened leaves
    that wrinkle to her soiled hands,
    though she barely flinches at the chill,
and at a campfire she heats away the frost.

We eat there, at the allotments,
the antioxidants like a doctor's medicine.
    My hand loosens
    on my boyfriend's shoulder,
        and he beams, as if he's felt tightness
        in my touch the whole week long.

Then he flexes his leg muscles.
Jumps.
            I can strangle you with these thighs,
            he laughs to me, and I laugh back,
while the veg lady makes off with the leftover leaf,
oddly shielding her neck.

DEBORAH FINDING

The Bride of Arta

In the Greek folk ballad, 'The Bridge of Arta', the Master
Builder and his team build a bridge across Arta's river, but it
collapses each night, until one day, a bird with a human voice
brings the news that, for it to stand, the Master Builder must
sacrifice his wife and build her into the foundations. The song
has a happy ending. This is her story.

He comes home red every night that summer
exhausted, angry, sweating out his frustration
with the gods. *We built it perfectly yet it crumbled
from the core AGAIN.* His punch cracks the plaster
but the wall stands firm. *My men must be laughing
at me. How can even YOU respect me as a man?*

I hold him like our newborn, shush-patting
his back until his breathing calms, his chest still,
before our proximity leads inevitably to him
distracting himself with my body, willingly given
over to the cause, our limbs rising and falling,
before collapsing into sleep. I begin to dream of crows.

He is quiet before he leaves, packed lunch in hand,
kissing our son's forehead. *Take care of your mother,*
he instructs our milk-drowsy baby. *Your father*

is building the bridge so you can walk over it
to explore and conquer the world, but your mother
will always be here, giving you a reason to return.

When I get the call that he needs me, I delay.
I want to stay nested in that tiny smile, the suckling,
such sweet need. But the birds are gathering,
those collective crows insisting it is time to go.
There is only one path to the bridge, and I take it.
He is there, master builder. My husband, my love.

My love, he says, not meeting my eyes, *I am so sorry,*
my ring has fallen into the foundations. He grips me,
his fingers tight talons on my arm. *I can't bear*
to be without it. You always find what I lose. Will you try?
His eyes are wet. I pretend I don't know why. Yes.
I reply. Yes. Of course I will. I would do anything for you.

The river runs shallow, once-nourished rushes
turning brown, past the point of no return,
jasmine twining up the wall, my wedding veil. I do.
I go down the pit, wonder how long it will take them
to lay the first brick. I swallow curses like wine
and change them to blessings. I do not speak again.

I caw cry for my hungry child. They tell the village
to stay away, that the bridge will not be safe for a week.
Even crows hold funerals for their dead.
But he comes every day. I recognise his footsteps,
hold my hands against the stone, imagine it warming
like my body would with his palms pressed against it.

I know he believes he would tear this bridge apart
if he hears just one sound from his beloved wife.
My final gift, last marriage act, is to not leave him
holding the knowledge that he would not.
I am silent until the reeds emerge from the rubble,
and after that, there is only birdsong.

My milk has become limestone, my shoulders steel
scaffolding, supporting all those who cross me.
I hold up the world for them, a familiar weight
to women used to bearing down, to descending
for love. My heart, the uncredited architect.
I know what my son will learn about heroes.

DEVJANI BODEPUDI

The guests we make

empty handed she painted
over our Renaissance skies

leaving them smudged on the bedroom floor.
She spoke with aching vowels

the colour and texture of open figs
forcing us to listen deeper.

She pressed her ear to ours and we heard gunfire
catching my grandmother as she fled

carved but loosely wrapped in six metres of widow white
coughing hibiscus blooms and brown feathers

we arranged on the kitchen windowsill
before lifting out fish bones from Rui

that night in a game. Trying not to stare
we followed the news

watching toads in monocles
with their buzzing throats

swollen with flies that hurt the quiet.
Grandmother taught us to sleep on the floor

while she lay lengthwise on the lid of her
steamer trunk by the wall.

She knew leaving too well. In the dark
I dreamt our guest un-hollowed herself

into the nacre of an empty shell
where laughter echoed and looped in silences

soaring away untethered into light years
weightlessness allowing for infinite height

imagining away from felled steel
glass and phosphorous grenades

while accidental corpses
shaped like her sister's children

once trapped under rubble floated up too
reminding her of dust motes in the sun.

Fitting one English verb into the space
behind her ribs when she woke

with wet eyes, we give her the infinitive to rise:
coaxing back her splintered tongue

a golden murmuration: a gift
readying itself for lasting defiance.

BRIDGETTE JAMES

The House of Refugees

Before I began straightening my hair with chemical relaxers from
    Dream Tresses
in Deptford, learnt to drop the 't' in Catford to sound more British
I inserted the keys into the lock of the Edwardian semi, beside the
    cemetery
and stepped into the House of Refugees. 'Soo dhawow' was how
    Woman One
greeted me – her smile the translator, she led me upstairs like an
    African Diplomat
to a child's single bedroom. I shared all the furniture in it with
    Woman Number Two.
Respecting house rules I left the traditional cloth draped over the
    full-length mirror
as if no one looks at reflections that don't mirror their true selves.
A shabby oakwood dresser housed the watermarked family photograph,
glass frame cracked into a myriad varicose veins. When I tried to
    show off
my knowledge about the Edwardian era of opulence and peace,
    Woman One told me
the man in photo, 'Never made it out of the dinghy.' I tried to muster
    up courage to ask,
'And your daughter?' Instead, gave her the tie-dyed blanket in my
    suitcase to introduce her

to my culture. To show people made and did not destroy before the
    war. When she
admired their handiwork, I told her how their ambidextrous hands
    'hacked off limbs,
ripped open wombs of expectant mothers, slaughtered children'. To
    Woman Two's
question, if I attended the primary school with the crucifix motif on
    the gate,
I replied, 'Same old story, but totally different country.' Because we
    needed
to trade stories when the downstairs TV broke and invent puzzles –
piecing the conundrum together why Ruth migrated to Israel.
Not all Ruths charm Boaz because Woman One came to the house
    with the hefty baggage
of weighted-down trauma of a child marriage. She gave me a jigsaw
    to piece together –
FGM. Unsolved, it hung like a garland from the ceiling in our shared
    space.
At Christmas, Woman One dipped generously into her benefits
    money,
treated us like princesses to shepherd's pie flavoured with spices
    Woman Two
kept in the kitchen cupboard, burned incense in place of mulberry
    candles.
Then I went upstairs to fetch my Bible from its pride of place on the
    shared drawer
next to the passport I had before my naturalisation, read the women
    this verse:
'For God so loved the world.'

MAX WALLIS

The second time

it was morphine made you love your cardboard hat:
perched upturned on your head until you needed it.
Of all the drugs you hated
that the most. It made you sick,
eyes at sea, and your arm like spam, swollen and taut:
cellulitis rooted deep. Still, you supped gin to top yourself up
straight from the bottle. Only convinced
to go to the hospital
when my brother, a doctor himself,
pointed out you might have sepsis so
the nurse would speed
you through.

They checked you over, hooked you up
to antibiotic flushes
and gave you morphine because nothing
else was enough.
You struggled to pee – both arms disabled,
one by machinery
and one by disease. I helped prop you
while you shuffled
to the toilet. And then you turned,
jerked, looked up
to the light, to the light, and then:

your eyes rolled back, and I
thought: not again.

For fuck's sake, please, not again,
and cupped my hand
behind your shaking head, and slammed myself into
the wall, so you'd slide against me instead. Your muscles
burning through their energy stores all at once.

And I yelled for a response,
while thirteen stone fell against me
and Wombat, I caught you, sort of –
do you remember that?
And your hand was frog-cold,
and wet to the touch.
Your sick-bowl hat
scuttling across the floor.

What's more, half a dozen doctors came,
asked your name,
while I reached for a pillow
and wedged my wallet into your mouth
in case your face bashed open like a peach
like it did in our flat.

And the doctors in coats
picked you up with a sheet,
injected the
anti-convulsing meds,
oxygen mask tight to your mouth.
I scrambled, picking up your stuff.

Then back to Resus again, bleep-bleep,
texting your parents to hurry, quick
to leave the dog in the flat, I don't care
and hurry, quick.
Cancel the holiday, hurry, quick.

And I
pleaded with the gay consultant to lie; scrub
your records clean, so they wouldn't know,
although they could plainly see
how much you drank or took

and while you haggled
with your life, coming to, seeing me,
smiling, then going back, *I* shook
and questioned mine
and questioned you.

And I helped the nurse to strip you. 'It's fine,'
I said. 'I've done this before.' And one
by one I bagged your piss-soaked clothes
to wash at home. And in that hospital
lie love's remains, in a ward
on Whitechapel Road.

JANE BURN

This Is Tree Time

The tree's long shadow moves around the day –
         noon is blossom.
I remember a time before I became invisible, when I was dating this guy
whose pet hate was

> *those people that take up all the room on the path,*
> *with their shopping in one hand and their walking sticks*
> *in the other – and you can't get past them.*
> *It's almost like they are walking that slowly*

> *on purpose.*   He said,
> *I want to shove them over.*

If he saw me now I bet he'd be really, really glad that we broke up.
Perhaps he has already tutted behind me on a pavement somewhere,
and didn't even recognise the woman that he used to say he loved –
perhaps he rolled his eyes, mimed the act of pushing me out of the way
to whoever he happened to be with.   He did this. I know.

Perhaps he would have scrambled over my back
         like an inconvenient bridge.

I tell the tree how I worry that I have become a ghost
         and this is why people walk at me
                  or through me, as if I'm not there.

Sometimes I make it an experiment – hold my ground,
instead of removing myself from their paths.

Sometimes there is a last-minute   *oh!*
Sometimes I am knocked to one side with a   bump
that hurts me for a while.
Sometimes the crowd parts around me
                        as if they were a river
                                and I a rock, spoiling its flow.

The world works its wheels around us.
Tree says   *s*   *l*   *o*   *w*   and *stay*
                                exactly as you are –
this is Tree Time.
        Imagine your stick is a root, planting you to the ground
    One o'clock is a page of birchbark,
        peeling, silver, written with light.

SUMAN GUJRAL

To an Ally

'How have you been?'
you asked

I hesitated, reluctant to reveal my hurts,
pain old and new
reverberating,
every atom remembering

but your eyes encouraged me;
I told you, my voice crying,
I told you, 'I have been injured'
another wound to my gentle soul

I trembled
in the silence
of the chance I'd taken,
curious, hopeful, undefended

'You have been bullied
this shouldn't happen
make a noise
this is not RIGHT'

'Easy for you to say,'
I thought
'some of us are WEARY
of this familiar fight'

you stepped up, though,
not a brace,
a shield,
you promised

'You don't have to do anything,
I will do it for you'

Layers of pain dispersed
by six words; I had not
known the weight of it
until you took my burden

I will do it for you

no hesitation, no further
questions, you opened
your heart to listen and
I began to heal

ABIGAIL OTTLEY

Transcript: Interview Room 2

Can I give you a description? No, not really. What part of
unseen are you struggling with? His face was always covered.
I never saw it. No distinguishing marks or scars. Look, our
whole lives were lived in the dark. No torches, candles or
mirrors. Not unkind exactly but he could be cold and
vengeful. You never quite knew what he was thinking. One
shade told me that, when he was like this, his behaviour was
just like his dad's. He did like to nuzzle at my neck like a
dog, though, and, sometimes, he would croon in my ear.
I know I shouldn't say this but I found that comforting. It
was better than being left alone. More often, his every word
was flinty. He chipped away at my confidence. Look, I've told
you everything. I'm hungry and exhausted. In Hera's name,
why would I lie? Of course I was afraid. I did struggle to
begin with, but he's enormous, much stronger than I am.
I know there are no fingerprints. Of course there aren't. He's
a bloody god. The best times were when he fed me strong,
sweet wine. My head spun and I couldn't feel my nose. There
was some herb in the wine. I don't know what. He said it
would help me forget. What else can I tell you? Only this.
His heart was carved from obsidian. It was so dark and hard
it reflected me back. It was home to screech owls and wolves.

CHRISTIAN WARD

Umbellifers

The Victorian ladies of yellow fennel
flowers on Ealing Common vie
for attention with the delicate lace
umbrellas of cow parsley. Coaches
of crows trundle along flattened paths,
eking out a meagre existence
from whatever earthworms corkscrew
their way upwards. Grandees
of horse chestnut trees prefer to hobnob
with their own sort, refusing saplings
of lesser varieties to nab sunlight.
Of course, you might glimpse that rarest
of things: common hogweed extending
its arms in a diplomatic gesture
hardly glimpsed among the red foxes
and badgers. The bumblebees
understand what needs to be done –
pollinating bridges for the peacock
butterfly strutting like a supermodel,
the noble house sparrow and the blackbird
offering its honesty among Instagrammable
wildflowers shedding stained-glass light
for camera-eyed ladybirds.

LAILA SUMPTON

We had a caravan

parked in the family tree, violin reels
tinting glass and prayers rising
like wood smoke to a mother and baby
decked in gold

before they sold those benediction eyes
to a priest who wondered
where the dealers roamed to next
with their black hair, their Pictish stance,
their dimpled wandering grins.

No one knows why they left,
readied their wagons
and carried tartan girls to the Humber
taking their names, their town-like ways
before putting out to sea.

Imported wives tapped cigarettes cold
and waited for ships to heel,
till they learnt that even their shadow
glancing the Albert Dock
could curse an entire crew.

Smart dressers with wonderful perms –
they watched through net curtains
for the strut of a ringside win,
laughing about how their boxers
took work home.

They dilute each year,
drift further from Romany roads
but clasp violins and keep a quiet fire
somewhere in their minds.
The routes they had taken

a palm line no one can read.
Their singing learnt, not absorbed,
the old name gone and trinity wilted
the day the nuns came knocking
begging a shilling for an empire

too used to the poor fearing –
but our Grandad refused,
never set foot under steeple again,
though he tended his Bible daily,
margins full, dog eared and whisky blurred.

When they scattered him in the Humber
to join his shipwrecked father
the priest marvelled at his faded verse –
'People don't read like this any more;
he had faith.'

REYZL GRACE

When I Open the Paper

for E.R. Shaffer

When I open the paper,
the earrings are spun
cotton. You
are proud of this –
call the fact
to my attention.

At the Museum of Russian
Art, I tugged you
towards a worker in overalls
and headscarf,
dressed with the promise
of the Revolution.

You listened patiently
as I babbled of a country
that unravelled before
I was grown, as I pulled
pilled Russian
from my pockets like lint.

But you watched, too –
didn't you? – as the blue
of her denim reflected
in my eyes… I snatch
at the memories of a hundred
years. A dozen

tongues drift through
my mouth like fallout –
wisps of stray
threshing on the wind
in the cotton fields
of Turkmenistan.

I twist after them,
naked in the breeze,
and tell you I am spinning.
I mean it to sound
futile – like men
mean it. Like tyres.

But you are a dervish,
and I – a woman.
When I open the paper,
I snatch at the wind
for words, babbling
Yiddish and Russian.

But I cannot repay
your gift with a gown
of *shatnez*, and I turn

into the space
between us, in need
of a new fibre

the wind has not carried
before. When I look
again at the earrings –
the tight wind
of the cotton – your teaching
opens. All

I have been
is beneath my fingers.
I am spinning. I am spinning.

ABOUT THE POETS

ANSUYA   *p. 50*

Ansuya spent her formative years in India but now considers herself a Londoner. She won the Geoff Stevens Memorial Poetry Prize 2024 and will have her collection published by Indigo Dreams next year. She was shortlisted for the Alpine and Aurora Poetry Prize in 2022, and was highly commended in the Erbacce 2024. Her poems have appeared in *Black in White*, *Drawn to the Light Press*, *Gypsophila*, *Ink Sweat & Tears*, *Last Stanza*, *Rattle*, *Third Space*, *Crowstep Journal*, *Cerasus*, *Artemesia Arts* and others.

STEVE BAGGS   *p. 20*

Steve Baggs is a poet and writer from Kent. Born in Deal, he now lives in Lewes. He has been published in several poetry magazines and is putting together his first collection of poetry. He has previously won a Co-Op Poetry Festival prize, and has performed his poetry across the country. He was once arrested for an impromptu poetry reading as part of a teenage guerrilla poetry night. Thankfully, it was all a misunderstanding! He enjoys writing haiku and has contributed to the *Time Haiku* magazine, and recently won second prize for a haibun he wrote.

KOUSHIK BANERJEA   *p. 30*

Koushik Banerjea is the author of two novels: *Another Kind of Concrete* and *Category Unknown*. His short stories have appeared in *Feign Lit, Jerry Jazz Musician, Salvation in Stereo, Minor Literatures, Verbal, Writers Resist* and in the crime fiction anthologies, *Shots in the Dark* and *Shots in the Dark II*. He has had poems published in *Third Space, Mogadored, Razur Cuts* magazine and online in *House of Poetry* magazine. His poem '*Sick Carnival*', a personal response to the racist riots which flared up across the UK in August 2024, was produced as a micro-chapbook by Scumbag Press. A former youth worker and DJ, he has also been a journalist, though try not to hold that against him. He lives in south London.

SEKHAR BANERJEE   *p. 93*

Sekhar Banerjee is from Jalpaiguri, an old tea town in sub-Himalayan West Bengal. A Pushcart Prize and Best of the Net Award-nominated poet, his work has been featured in various publications, such as *Stand Magazine, Poetry Wales, Arkana, Ink Sweat & Tears and The Lake*. Sekhar is the author of two poetry collections, *The Fern Gatherer's Association* and *Probably Geranium*. Currently residing in Kolkata, India, Sekhar has a passion for remote places, tea and mobile photography. The title, 'Sources for the History of Bhutan', pays tribute to British Tibetologist Michael Aris, who extensively worked on Bhutan's history and authored a book with the same title.

HEINRICH BEINDORF   *p. 24*

Hailing from a small German coal-mining town, Heinrich studied languages and literature in Munich,

Toronto and the USSR before settling down in Cologne
as a translator and author. His poetry and short prose
have appeared in magazines and anthologies as well as
on radio and the web.

REBECCA G. BIBER   *p. 37*

Rebecca G. Biber is a collaborative pianist and music
teacher living in Ann Arbor, Michigan. Her poetry has
appeared in *Lilith*, *Delmar*, *The Passionfruit Review*, *The Petigru
Review*, *RE:AL* and the forthcoming *Bop, Strut, and Dance
Anthology*. Her first book of poems, *Technical Solace*, was
published in 2017 by Fifth Avenue Press.

ALISON BINNEY   *p. 17*

Alison Binney is a poet and English teacher from Cambridge.
Her debut pamphlet, *Other Women's Kitchens*, won the Mslexia
Pamphlet Competition and was published by Seren Books
in 2021. She has a full collection forthcoming with Seren
Books in spring 2025.

DEVJANI BODEPUDI   *p. 101*

Devjani Bodepudi is a British Indian poet. Her work has
appeared in several publications including *Dust Poetry
Mag*, *The Hooghly Review* and the *Third Space* anthology
published by Renard Press. Her debut poetry pamphlet
won a Saboteur Award in 2023. Devjani holds an MA in
Creative Writing from the University of Birmingham and
is pursuing a PhD at Manchester Metropolitan University,
examining the complexities and poetics of the impact of
a lost language on identity.

CREANA BOSAC   *p. 22*

Creana Bosac lives in Leicestershire, where she has worked
as an Associate Lecturer in Ecology for the Open University.
Having written mainly scientific documents before, she enjoys
writing creatively, especially about the natural world and
neurodiversity issues. Her work has appeared in *Lucent Dreaming*,
Briefly Zine and *The Storms* amongst others, and she has authored
a creative writing feedback guide. She particularly likes plants
and being in the outdoors.

JANE BURN   *p. 108*

Jane Burn is an award-winning, working-class poet, artist and
hybrid writer, with autism. Her work is widely published and
anthologised. Her current collection, *The Apothecary of Flight*, is
published by Nine Arches. She is the Michael Marks Awards
Environmental Poet of the Year 2023–24.

RACHEL BURNS   *p. 76*

Rachel Burns lives in County Durham and is a poet, short story
writer and playwright. She has been placed in poetry competitions
including The Julian Lennon Prize for Poetry and The Classical
Association Poetry Competition. She lives with a disability and
chronic illness and is a support worker for a homeless charity.

MARÍA CASTRO DOMÍNGUEZ   *p. 74*

María Castro Domínguez is the author of *A Face in The Crowd*,
her Erbacce-winning collection, and *Ten Truths from Wonderland*, a
collaboration with Matt Duggan. In 2023 she won first prize in
The Plaza Poetry Prize, and was a runner-up in The Red Shed
Poetry Comp 2024. Previously she won third prize in Brittle Star's
Poetry Competition 2018. Her poems have appeared in many

anthologies and journals, including *Popshot, PANK, Empty Mirror, The Lincoln Review, The Friday Poem, Orbis, Chattahoochee Review, The Cortland Review* and *Backlash Press.* She's a philologist and freelance writer, passionate about words and how they communicate.

VICTORIA D'CRUZ   *p. 73*

Victoria D'Cruz studied poetry at Stirling University, where she was inspired by Jackie Kay. Her forthcoming first collection of poetry, which she regularly performs, is called *The Zebra Crossing.* It explores racism and the perspective of being mixed race. Victoria is a former BBC journalist, who now works as a digital content editor for a global brand. In between raising two children and redrafting her first novel, she dreams of having a room of her own to write in.

DELILAH DENNETT   *p. 64*

Delilah Dennett is a writer and performer. Her work has previously been featured in *Heroica, The Dial* and *West Trade Review.* She is a graduate of the New Earth Theatre Writers Academy as well as the New Earth Theatre Performers Academy. Dennett recently participated in the Roundhouse Centre 59 Performance Academy, curated by actor Daniel Kaluuya, where she performed an original spoken-word piece called 'The Part that Stayed' in the final showcase.

ALICE EAVES   *p. 79*

Alice Eaves is a writer and PhD Researcher at the University of Edinburgh. She is Editor of *Tiny Flames: Voices from Ukraine,* featured on BBC Scotland. 'Our Lady Star of the Sea' was first published in film form with thanks to Geelong Regional Libraries & Melbourne City of Literature, 2024.

GERALD EWA   *p. 61*

Ewa Gerald Onyebuchi is an Igbo storyteller from Nigeria. He writes short stories, essays and poetry. In 2023, he was longlisted for the Abubakar Gimba Prize for Creative Non-Fiction, the Brigitte Porson Prize for literature, and was a finalist in the Gerald Kraak Prize 2023. He has been published in *Ubwali, Isele, Efiko, Decolonial Passage* and elsewhere.

DEBORAH FINDING   *p. 98*

Deborah Finding is a queer feminist writer with a background in academia and activism. She is the author of two poetry pamphlets: *Vigils for Dead and Dying Girls* (Nine Pens) and *Amortisation* (Live Canon), and has a collection forthcoming with Write Bloody UK. Her other publications include *Propel, fourteen poems*, the *Guardian*, *DIVA*, *berlin lit* and *Anthropocene*. Deborah won the Write By The Sea, Live Canon and Indigo Dreams poetry competitions, and has been placed, commended, or shortlisted in many others. Originally from the North-East, Deborah now lives in London, where she is poet in residence at the Soho Poly.

REYZL GRACE   *p. 116*

Reyzl Grace is an Ashkenazi Russian American writer, librarian and translator working in English, Yiddish and Russian. A past Pushcart nominee and contributor to *Room, Rust & Moth, So to Speak* and other periodicals, she is also a current poetry editor for *Psaltery & Lyre* and an incorrigible lesbian. Originally from Alaska, she now lives in Minneapolis with her novelist girlfriend, arguing over which of them is the better writer. (It's her girlfriend.)

CARL GRIFFIN   *p. 95*

Carl Griffin is a writer from Swansea, south Wales. His latest book is the long poem *Arrival at Elsewhere*, a collaborative poem published by Against the Grain Press.

SUMAN GUJRAL   *p. 110*

Suman Gujral is a multidisciplinary artist working with print, textile and poetry. She has an MA in Fine Art, specialising in printmaking. Suman's history as a child of refugees and immigrants underlies her practice. Her parents were forcibly displaced by the 1947 Partition of India, and came to the UK eighteen years later. It was during her MA that she came to understand the ongoing impact of Partition on them and millions of others. The cycle of war and displacement, rooted in colonial action, which un-homed her parents, continues across the globe today. She feels that as an artist, she's in a unique position to cast a light on these difficult subjects. She is fascinated by human ability to survive and even thrive, in the aftermath of traumatic events. Community engagement is central to her practice.

KINSHUK GUPTA   *p. 125*

Kinshuk Gupta is a bilingual writer, poet and translator who works at the intersection of gender, health and sexuality. His debut book of short fiction, *Yeh Dil Hai Ki Chordarwaja*, Hindi's first modern LGBTQ+ short-story collection, was published to great critical acclaim in 2023. He is the winner of prestigious awards, including the India Today-Aaj Tak Sahitya Jagriti Udayiman Lekhak Samman (2023); Akhil Bhartiya Yuva Kathakar Alankaran (2022); and Dr Anamika Poetry Prize (2021). He has been shortlisted for the Toto Awards for Creative Writing (2023); The Bridport Prize (2022); Srinivas Rayparol Poetry

Prize (2021); and All India Poetry Competition (2018). His work has appeared or is forthcoming in *Rattle*, *adda*, *On the Edge* and *Late-Blooming Cherries: Haiku Poets from India*, among others. He has been awarded the South Asia Speaks 2023 Fellowship to work on his poetry manuscript with Tishani Doshi.

OZ HARDWICK   *p. 19*

Oz Hardwick is a European poet, photographer, barely competent bass guitarist and accidental academic, who has been described as a 'major proponent of the neo-surreal prose poem in Britain'. His most recent full collection, *A Census of Preconceptions*, was shortlisted for a number of international awards but didn't win any, though he feels pretty confident about the upcoming egg-and-spoon race. His latest publications include the chapbook *Retrofuturism for the Dispossessed* and a track on the *Aliens Within* picture disc by space rockers Incubus Lovechild. Oz is Professor of Creative Writing at Leeds Trinity University.

SHEENA HUSSAIN   *p. 41*

Sheena Hussain is a British Pakistani poet, writer and essayist, and is a non-practising immigration lawyer who turned to poetry after receiving a cancer diagnosis. 'No Thanks', a creative non-fiction piece, was shortlisted for the inaugural Curae Prize 2023. 'Watching a Green Fly' was longlisted for the Leeds Poetry Festival Competition 2022. She is widely anthologised and is the founder of Poem:99, an international children's poetry competition. She is a member of Inscribe-Peepal Tree Press's writer's development programme. When not writing poetry, you will find her hiking up mountains and taking long solitary walks.

LJ IRETON   *p. 48*

LJ Ireton is a vegan poet and a bookseller from London. Her poems have been published by numerous journals both in print and online, including *Green Ink Poetry*, *Spellbinder Literary Magazine*, *Spelt* and *Wild Greens Magazine*, and in the printed anthologies *Spectrum* and *York Literary Review 2023*. Her debut poetry collection, *Lessons from the Sky*, was published by Ellipsis Imprints in 2024. Her second collection, *Interlude*, will be published by Haywood Books in 2025.

BRIDGETTE JAMES   *p. 103*

Bridgette James is a British writer born in Sierra Leone. Her poem won the Flash Fiction Summer Poem 2024. She was shortlisted for the Bridport 2024 and longlisted for the Aurora Prize for Writing 2022. She was a Metropolitan Police Special Constable.

POET THE JULES   *p. 127*

poet the jules is a writer, actor, artist and performer extraordinaire. You name it, and they have probably thought about creating it. Growing up in Germany with a love for poetry and theatre, they moved to London to pursue a creative career. Jules is an Anthroplay Associate Artist, and their work was showcased on the BBC, in Tate Britain, and in various esteemed magazines and publications. They are a regular feature of the local open-mic scene, and they thoroughly enjoy experimenting with performance poetry. Their favourite things include rubber ducks, sunsets, crochet snails, oatmeal and comparing the universe to soup.

TIM KIELY   *p. 58*

Tim Kiely is a criminal barrister and writer based in London. His poetry and critical writing has appeared in *Under the Radar*, *Impossible Archetype*, *Magma* and *Ink, Sweat & Tears*, and in anthologies from the Emma Press, Broken Sleep Books, Renard Press, the Ginkgo Prize for Ecopoetry and the Verve Poetry Festival Competition. He is a member of Poetry on the Picket Line and has contributed to the work of Poets for the Planet. He is the author of three poetry pamphlets, including *Hymn to the Smoke* and *No Other Life*.

DULANI KULASINGHE   *p. 39*

Dulani Kulasinghe is a writer and educator whose creative practice explores belonging, contested histories and legacies of empire. Her writing is supported by Writing Our Legacy and Arts Council England and has been published and anthologised widely. Dulani's site-responsive work includes poems about the Chattri Memorial for Brighton Festival and the presence of Caribbean soldiers in WWI Seaford. Her writing is taught at Sussex University and she runs writing workshops for young people and adults; she is also involved in anti-racist curriculum change. Dulani is a New Writing South:21 Fellow and lives in Brighton with her family.

MARK LAVERY   *p. 33*

Mark Lavery was born in Canada, the youngest son of a Scottish father and a Bermudian mother. A lover of adventure, he spent time living and working in all three countries before finally settling in the land of his father in 2019. With degrees in Political Science, Theatre and Law, Mark's work often explores the tension between power and vulnerability, reflecting his fascination with the forces and narratives that shape our world. A proud father of three, he balances his newly sparked literary pursuits with the joys and chaos of family life in Glasgow.

LINNEA   *p. 81*

Linnea is a film student and at-home writer. They've had their poetry published by the6ress, won the Dan Hemingway award for their collection *Home*, and been longlisted for the *Indigo Teen Magazine*. They're working on their second novel and hope to one day have a published book and a dog (funded by the book), but will continue reading, writing, baking and learning about activism in the mean time.

PIPPA LITTLE   *p. 47*

Pippa Little is Scots, born in Tanzania and now settled in Northumberland in England. She is a poetry tutor for the Faber Academy, a mentor, editor and reviewer with three full collections and four pamphlets. Her work has won awards and is widely anthologised.

JASPREET MANDER   *p. 129*

Jaspreet Mander was born in Punjab, India. Having studied English literature and language, she lectured at her alma mater, Punjabi University, Patiala. In 2022, she completed MA in Creative Writing at Leeds Trinity University. Her collections of poetry include *Lemons Oranges & Pomegranates*, *Our Land Our Times* and *Tawny Glows*. In England, her writings have been published in *Dream Catcher*, *Shine*, *Wordspace* anthologies, *Hear Me Now* Volume Two and *Third Space*. Her radio programmes are available on east Leeds' Chapel FM website.

MWENDIA MURIITHI   *p. 71*

Mwendia is a young poet from Cambridgeshire. She writes about the world around her and how it interacts with her as a young black woman. In recent years, Mwendia has performed at various fundraisers and grassroots festivals including a Gala for Gaza and the annual Core 4 Cultural Fashion show. She has Kenyan heritage, of which she is very proud and passionate about. Other published poems by her include 'The Odd Space in Between' and 'You Ain't Really Serious'.

GEETHA NAIR G.   *p. 67*

Geetha Nair G., a former Associate Professor of English, All Saints' College, Thiruvananthapuram, is the author of two collections of poetry, *Shored Fragments* and *Drawing Flame*, and two collections of short fiction. Her work has been widely published in journals and anthologies of note. She has compiled and co-edited three international anthologies of short fiction. Geetha Nair is the CEO of Folio Publishers, a publishing concern based in Thiruvananthapuram, Kerala, India.

YUKTI NARANG   *p. 35*

Yukti Narang is an emerging Indian creative writer, screenwriter and dramatist. Her work has appeared in literary magazines including *Room*, *Aniko Press*, *Oh Reader*, *The Chiron Review*, *Ekstasis* and *Sunday Mornings at the River*, and her short fiction is part of upcoming anthologies by *Rupa Publications India*, *The Blaft Book of Anti-Caste SF* and elsewhere. Her debut poetry collection, *There Is a Home in All of Us*, was published in 2023. Yukti is currently creating new literary and screen works. She is working to make it big in literature and cinema and wants to be a versatile storyteller.

HANA ORMARA   *p. 62*

Hana Ormara is a British poet whose work has been
published by the International Human Rights Arts
Movement (IHRAM), UCL's Writer's Block Magazine and
in the *Third Space* anthology. Her writing is influenced by
her Baloch heritage and its indigenous traditions of poetry
and storytelling through spoken word. In 'Legends of the
Sun: A Hybrid Ghazal of Migration', Hana's poem in
Building Bridges, the symbol of the sun, which represents an
unconquerable life force, was inspired by her late father, and
it pays homage to the bravery and lives of migrants.

ABIGAIL OTTLEY   *p. 112*

Abigail Ottley writes poetry and short fiction. Her work has
featured in more than 250 magazines and journals, most
recently in *Twisted Ink* and *Inkfish*. This year, she placed
second in the Plaza Prose Poem Competition and won the
Wildfire 150 Flash Award for the second year running. Twice
commended in The Page Is Printed and commended in the
Welshpool and *What We Inherit From Water*, she is presently
shortlisted for the Patricia Eschen Poetry Prize. Abigail lives
in Penzance, where she is a member of the all-female Mor
Poet Collective. Her debut collection, *Out of Eden*, will be
published by Yaffles Nest in May 2025.

SUCHITA PARIKH-MUNDUL   *p. 69*

Suchita Parikh-Mundul works as a writer and copy editor in
Mumbai, India. Some of her articles can be read online at
The Swaddle. Her poetry has appeared in *The Bombay Literary
Magazine*, Sahitya Akademi's *Indian Literature*, *Usawa Literary
Review*, *Outlook India* and various anthologies.

IVY RAFF   *p. 43*

Ivy Raff is the author of *What Remains*, which won the Alberola International Poetry Prize, and *Rooted and Reduced to Dust*. Her *Best of the Net*-nominated poems appear in *Ninth Letter,* Electric Literature's *The Commuter* and *West Trade Review*, among numerous others, as well as in the anthologies *London Independent Story Prize Anthology* 2023 and *Aesthetica Creative Writing Prize Annual* 2023. Ivy serves artist communities as MacDowell's Senior Systems Project Manager and as a member of *Seventh Wave Magazine*'s editorial team.

EMILY REYNOLDS   *p. 52*

Emily Reynolds is a poet from Bristol, England. She has poems published in *Bloody Amazing* and *Locked In* anthologies and several journals. When she's not writing Emily is working with new parents in north Bristol and moving increasingly heavy weights in the gym.

DAPHNE SAMPSON   *p. 54*

Daphne Sampson was born in north London in 1950, and started reading poetry as a moon-struck teenager. After growing up in Kent she worked in two wonderfully creative primary schools off the Old Kent Road, previously only known to her as that brown Monopoly card, the cheapest on the board. This vibrant community had some of the exhilaration of the first plunge of a wild swim. She taught for two years in Kenya, something that nourished her love of the natural world. Later in Norfolk with her young family Daphne became involved in environmental campaigning. She had a severe stroke in 2021.

KAY SAUNDERS *p. 91*

Kay Saunders is a young woman from the Cotswolds who has been writing creatively her whole life. A core source of her inspiration has come from her experiences within the LGBT+ community, which empowers her to create heartfelt narratives that are relatable and a safe place for people to feel seen and understood. Between short stories, flash fiction and poetry, Kay has won local awards for her writing and recognition from publishers and authors, and hopes to soon join her literary idols in a world of publication as she works on her first novel.

THEA SMILEY *p. 32*

Thea Smiley is a Suffolk-based poet. In 2024, her work was shortlisted for The Frogmore Prize and the Second Light Competition. Her poems have been widely published in magazines and anthologies, shortlisted for the Bridport Prize, and longlisted in the Rialto Nature and Place competition. 'As the Last Song Begins to Play' was written for Tom and Zoë.

ALYSON SMITH *p. 78*

Based in Newcastle upon Tyne, Alyson Smith is a working-class writer and artist who has Bi-Polar and Level I Autism. She works as an administrator in a nursing home and has recently received her MA in Creative Writing from the Open University. Alyson has had poems published in anthologies by Renard Press and is a regular contributor of short stories in Pagans of the North's monthly online magazine.

SUJATHA MENON *p. 84*

Sujatha Menon is a writer and musician based in the Midlands, and editor of *Crowstep Poetry Journal*. Her third collection forthcoming with Pindrop Press stems from a two-year poetry residency at the University of Warwick, where she has been helping to promote women in science. Her songs with the band Satsangi have been regularly broadcast on BBC radio and have featured on MTV and in *Rolling Stone* magazine.

LAILA SUMPTON *p. 114*

Laila Sumpton is a poet, editor, performer and educator who works with schools, hospitals, museums and charities on a wide variety of poetry projects. She co-founded the reparative education organisation Poetry vs. Colonialism and is an associate artist with intergenerational charity Magic Me. Laila's poetry has been published in numerous magazines and anthologies, including *Third Space*.

MAX WALLIS *p. 105*

Max Wallis is a poet, journalist and writer. He is the Polari Prize-shortlisted author of *Modern Love*. He is also a recovering addict and alcoholic and lives in Lancashire, where he is rebuilding his life slowly after a suicide attempt in February 2024. He is thirty-five.

CHRISTIAN WARD *p. 134*

Christian Ward is a UK-based poet with two collections, *Intermission* and *Zoo*, available on Amazon and elsewhere. His work has appeared in numerous literary journals, was longlisted for the 2023 National Poetry Competition and has been recognised this year in the Ware, Maria Edgeworth, Pen to Print, London Independent Story and Shahidah Janjua poetry competitions.

DAVE WYNNE-JONES   *p. 45*

Dave Wynne-Jones spent twenty years in teaching before leaving for health reasons, gaining an MA in creative writing at MMU and publishing *Kidstuff*, a collection of poems to share with children. He then scratched a living, writing articles for outdoor magazines and organising expeditions for mountaineers. Whittles have published his two mountaineering non-fiction books, *4000m Climbing the Highest Mountains of the Alps* and *An Expedition Handbook*. A Taoist poetry pamphlet, *The Way Taken*, published by Delfryn, is based on his first expedition to China. His poetry has also been anthologised and appeared in magazines like *Orbis* and *PN Review*.

There was originally another poem on the shortlist, but sadly we were unable to include the poem in this edition.

SUPPORTERS

This project was made possible through the financial support of the kind people listed below (in alphabetical order).

Kristin Bartlett
Michèle Clement
Matt Dady-Leonard
Deborah Finding
Ellie Herda-Grimwood
Peter Hill
Bridgette O James
Nadia Lazazi
George Lowden
Jaspreet Mander
Sujatha Menon
Abigail Rowland
Shivdular Singh Dhillon
Lorna Smart
Simon Wallis and Anne Stafford
Dave Wynne-Jones

A NOTE ON SUSTAINABILITY

RENARD PRESS feels strongly that there is no denying the climate crisis, and we all have a part to play in fixing the problem.

We are proud to be one of the UK's first climate-positive publishers, taking more carbon out of the air than we put in. How? We reduce our emissions as much as possible, using green energy, printing locally and choosing the materials we use carefully; we calculate our carbon footprint and doubly offset it through gold-standard schemes; and we plant a tree for every order we receive via our website to give back to the planet.

Find out more at:

RENARDPRESS.COM/ECO